The Sonnets by William Lisle Bowles

William Lisle Bowles was born on 24th September 1762 at King's Sutton in Northamptonshire.

His great-grandfather, grandfather and his father, William Thomas Bowles, had all been parish priests and inevitably Bowles would join their line.

In 1789 Bowles published, a small quarto volume, Fourteen Sonnets, which was received with extraordinary praise, not only by the general public, but by such revered poets as Samuel Taylor Coleridge and Wordsworth.

After receiving his degree at Oxford, Bowles now began his career in service to the Church of England.

His years of service perhaps diminished both his stature as a poet and certainly the way he was viewed. For much of his career Bowles was seen as rather soft when set against his contemporaries but in the end his ability as a poet was enshrined, after a long and ferocious attack against him, by the principles he so eloquently wrote about and adhered too.

In personality and nature Bowles was said to be an amiable, absent-minded, but rather eccentric man. His poems speak warmly of a refinement of feeling, tenderness, and pensive thought, but are lacking in power and passion. But that should not diminish their value or appreciation to us.

Bowles maintained that images drawn from nature are poetically finer than those drawn from art; and that in the highest kinds of poetry the themes or passions handled should be of the general or elemental kind, and not the transient manners of any society.

As well as his poetry Bowles was also responsible for writing a Life of Bishop Ken (in two volumes, 1830–1831), Coombe Ellen and St. Michael's Mount (1798), The Battle of the Nile (1799), and The Sorrows of Switzerland (1801).

William Lisle Bowles died on April 7th, 1850 at the age of 87.

Index of Contents

Preface
Introduction to the Edition of 1837
SONNETS
At Tynemouth Priory, after a Tempestuous Voyage
Bamborough Castle
The River Wainsbeck
The Tweed Visited
On leaving a Village in Scotland
Evening
To the River Itchin
On Resigning a Scholarship of Trinity College, Oxford, and Retiring to a Country Curacy
Dover Cliffs

On Landing at Ostend
The Bells of Ostend
The Rhine
Influence of Time on Grief
The Convent
The River Cherwell
On Entering Switzerland
Distant View of England from the Sea
Hope
To a Friend
Absence
Bereavement
Oxford Revisited
In Memoriam
On the Death of the Rev. William Benwell, M.A.
At Malvern
Netley Abbey
Associations
Music
Approach of Summer
At Oxford, 1786
At Dover, 1786
Retrospection
On Accidentally Meeting a Lady, now no more
On hearing "The Messiah" performed in Gloucester Cathedral, Sept. 18, 1835
Woodspring Abbey, 1836
Lacock Nunnery, 1837
On a Beautiful Landscape
Art and Nature: the Bridge between Clifton and Leigh Woods
Picture of an Old Man
Picture of a Young Lady
Hour-glass and Bible
Milton. Two Sonnets on the bust of Milton, in Youth and Age, at Stourhead
To Sir Walter Scott
William Lisle Bowles – A Short Biography

PREFACE

A Ninth Edition of the following Poems having been called for by the public, the author is induced to say a few words, particularly concerning those which, under the name of Sonnets, describe his personal feelings.

They can be considered in no other light than as exhibiting occasional reflections which naturally arose in his mind, chiefly during various excursions, undertaken to relieve, at the time, depression of spirits. They were, therefore, in general, suggested by the scenes before them; and wherever such scenes appeared to harmonise with his disposition at the moment, the sentiments were involuntarily prompted.

Numberless poetical trifles of the same kind have occurred to him, when perhaps, in his solitary rambles, he has been "chewing the cud of sweet and bitter fancy;" but they have been forgotten as he left the places which gave rise to them; and the greater part of those originally committed to the press were written down, for the first time, from memory.

This is nothing to the public; but it may serve in some measure to obviate the common remark on melancholy poetry, that it has been very often gravely composed, when possibly the heart of the writer had very little share in the distress he chose to describe.

But there is a great difference between natural and fabricated feelings, even in poetry. To which of these two characters the poems before the reader belong, the author leaves those who have felt sensations of sorrow to judge.

They who know him, know the occasions of them to have been real; to the public he might only mention the sudden death of a deserving young woman, with whom,

... Sperabatlongosheu! ducere soles,
Et fidoacclinisconsenuissesinu.[1]

DONHEAD, April 1805.

[1] The early editions of these Sonnets, 1791, were dedicated to the Reverend Newton Ogle, D.D., Dean of Winchester.

INTRODUCTION TO THE EDITION OF 1837

To account for the variations which may be remarked in this last edition of my Sonnets, from that which was first published fifty years ago, it may be proper to state, that to the best of my recollection, they now appear nearly as they were originally composed in my solitary hours; when, in youth a wanderer among distant scenes, I sought forgetfulness of the first disappointment in early affections.

Delicacy even now, though the grave has long closed over the beloved object, would forbid entering on a detail of the peculiar circumstances in early life, and the anguish which occasioned these poetical meditations. In fact, I never thought of writing them down at the time, and many had escaped my recollection;[2] but three years after my return to England, on my way to the banks of Cherwell, where

"I bade the pipe farewell, and that sad lay
Whose music, on my melancholy way,
I wooed,"

passing through Bath, I wrote down all I could recollect of these effusions, most elaborately mending the versification from the natural flow of music in which they occurred to me, and having thus corrected and written them out, took them myself to the late Mr Cruttwell, with the name of "Fourteen Sonnets, written chiefly on Picturesque Spots during a Journey."

I had three times knocked at this amiable printer's door, whose kind smile I still recollect; and at last, with much hesitation, ventured to unfold my message; it was to inquire whether he would give any thing for "Fourteen Sonnets," to be published with or without the name.[3] He at once declined the purchase, and informed me he doubted very much whether the publication would repay the expense of printing, which would come to about five pounds. It was at last determined one hundred copies, in quarto, should be published as a kind of "forlorn hope;" and these "Fourteen Sonnets" I left to their fate and thought no more of getting rich by poetry! In fact, I owed the most I ever owed at Oxford, at this time, namely, seventy pounds;[4] and knowing my father's large family and trying circumstances, and those of my poor mother, I shrunk from asking more money when I left home, and went back with a heavy heart to Oxford, under the conscious weight, that my poetic scheme failing, I had no means of paying Parsons, the mercer's, bill! This was the origin of the publication.

As this plain account is so connected with whatever may be my name in criticism and poetry, it is hoped it will be pardoned.

All thoughts of succeeding as a poet were now abandoned; but, half a year afterwards, I received a letter from the printer informing me that the hundred copies were all sold, adding, that if I had published FIVE HUNDRED copies, he had no doubt they would have been sold also.

This, in my then situation, my father now dead, and my mother a widow with seven children, and with a materially reduced income (from the loss of the rectories of Uphill and Brean in Somerset), was gratifying indeed; all my golden dreams of poetical success were renewed;—the number of the sonnets first published was increased, and five hundred copies, by the congratulating printer, with whose family I have lived in kindest amity from that hour, were recommended to issue from the press of the editor of the Bath Chronicle.

But this was not all, the five hundred copies were sold to great advantage, for it was against my will that five hundred copies should be printed, till the printer told me he would take the risk on himself, on the usual terms, at that time, of bookseller and author.

Soon afterwards, it was agreed that seven hundred and fifty copies should be printed, in a smaller and elegant size. I had received Coleridge's warm testimony; but soon after this third edition came out, my friend, Mr Cruttwell, the printer, wrote a letter saying that two young gentlemen, strangers, one a particularly handsome and pleasing youth, lately from Westminster School, and both literary and intelligent, spoke in high commendation of my volume, and if I recollect right, expressed a desire to have some poems printed in the same type and form. Who these young men were I knew not at the time, but the communication of the circumstance was to me most gratifying; and how much more gratifying, when, from one of them, after he himself had achieved the fame of one of the most virtuous and eloquent of the writers in his generation, I received a first visit at my parsonage in Wiltshire upwards of forty years afterwards! It was ROBERT SOUTHEY. We parted in my garden last year, when stealing time and sorrow had marked his still manly, but most interesting countenance.[5]—Therefore,

TO ROBERT SOUTHEY, WHO HAS EXHIBITED IN HIS PROSE WORKS, AS IN HIS LIFE, THE PURITY AND VIRTUES OF ADDISON AND LOCKE, AND IN HIS POETRY THE IMAGINATION AND SOUL OF SPENSER, THESE POEMS, WITH EVERY AFFECTIONATE PRAYER, ARE INSCRIBED BY
HIS SINCERE FRIEND,
WILLIAM LISLE BOWLES.

[2] I confined myself to fourteen lines, because fourteen lines seemed best adapted to unity of sentiment. I thought nothing about the strict Italian model; the verses naturally flowed in unpremeditated harmony, as my ear directed, but the slightest inspection will prove they were far from being mere elegiac couplets. The subjects were chiefly from river scenery, and the reader will recollect what Sir Humphrey Davy has said on this subject so beautifully; it will be recollected, also, that they were published ten years before those of Mr Wordsworth on the river Duddon, Yarrow, et cet. There have been many claimants, among modern poets, for the laurel of the sonnet, but, in picturesque description, sentiment, and harmony, I know none superior to those of my friend the Rev. Charles Hoyle, on scenery in Scotland, the mountains of Ben Nevis, Loch Lomond, et cet.

[3] To account for the present variations, some remained as originally with their natural pauses, others for the press I thought it best to correct into verse less broken, and now, after fifty years, they are recorrected, and restored, I believe, more nearly to the original shape in which they were first meditated.

[4] I hoped by my Sonnets to pay this vast debt.

[5] His companion, Mr Lovel, died in youth.

SONNETS

AT TYNEMOUTH PRIORY, AFTER A TEMPESTUOUS VOYAGE [6]

As slow I climb the cliff's ascending side,
Much musing on the track of terror past,
When o'er the dark wave rode the howling blast,
Pleased I look back, and view the tranquil tide
That laves the pebbled shore: and now the beam
Of evening smiles on the gray battlement,
And yon forsaken tower that time has rent:—
The lifted oar far off with transient gleam
Is touched, and hushed is all the billowy deep!
Soothed by the scene, thus on tired Nature's breast
A stillness slowly steals, and kindred rest;
While sea-sounds lull her, as she sinks to sleep,
Like melodies that mourn upon the lyre,
Waked by the breeze, and, as they mourn, expire!

[6] The remains of this monastery are situated on a lofty point, on the north side of the entrance into the river Tyne, about a mile and a half below North Shields. The rock on which the monastery stood rendered

it visible at sea a long way off, in every direction, whence it presented itself as if exhorting the seamen in danger to make their vows, and promise masses and presents to the Virgin Mary and St Oswin for their deliverance.

BAMBOROUGH CASTLE [7]

Ye holy Towers that shade the wave-worn steep,
Long may ye rear your aged brows sublime,
Though, hurrying silent by, relentless Time
Assail you, and the winds of winter sweep
Round your dark battlements; for far from halls
Of Pride, here Charity hath fixed her seat,
Oft listening, tearful, when the tempests beat
With hollow bodings round your ancient walls;
And Pity, at the dark and stormy hour
Of midnight, when the moon is hid on high,
Keeps her lone watch upon the topmost tower,
And turns her ear to each expiring cry;
Blessed if her aid some fainting wretch may save,
And snatch him cold and speechless from the wave.

[7] This ancient castle, with its extensive domains, heretofore the property of the family of Forster, whose heiress married Lord Crewe, Bishop of Durham, is appropriated by the will of that pious prelate to many benevolent purposes; particularly to that of administering instant relief to such shipwrecked mariners as may happen to be cast upon this dangerous coast; for whose preservation and that of their vessels every possible assistance is contrived, and is at all times ready. The estate is in the hands of trustees appointed under the Bishop's will.

THE RIVER WAINSBECK [8]

While slowly wanders thy sequestered stream,
WAINSBECK, the mossy-scattered rocks among,
In fancy's ear making a plaintive song
To the dark woods above, that waving seem
To bend o'er some enchanted spot, removed
From life's vain coil; I listen to the wind,
And think I hear meek Sorrow's plaint, reclined
O'er the forsaken tomb of him she loved!—
Fair scenes, ye lend a pleasure, long unknown,
To him who passes weary on his way;—
Yet recreated here he may delay
A while to thank you; and when years have flown,
And haunts that charmed his youth he would renew,
In the world's crowd he will remember you.

[8] The Wainsbeck is a sequestered river in Northumberland, having on its banks "Our Lady's Chapel," three-quarters of a mile west of Bothal. It has been commemorated by Akenside.

THE TWEED VISITED

O Tweed! a stranger, that with wandering feet
O'er hill and dale has journeyed many a mile,
(If so his weary thoughts he might beguile),
Delighted turns thy stranger-stream to greet.
The waving branches that romantic bend
O'er thy tall banks a soothing charm bestow;
The murmurs of thy wandering wave below
Seem like the converse of some long-lost friend.
Delightful stream! though now along thy shore,
When spring returns in all her wonted pride,
The distant pastoral pipe is heard no more;[9]
Yet here while laverocks sing could I abide,
Far from the stormy world's contentious roar,
To muse upon thy banks at eventide.

[9] Alluding to the simple and affecting pastoral strains for which Scotland has been so long celebrated. I need not mention Lochaber, the Braes of Bellendine, Tweedside, et cet.

ON LEAVING A VILLAGE IN SCOTLAND

Clysdale! as thy romantic vales I leave,
And bid farewell to each retiring hill,
Where musing memory seems to linger still,
Tracing the broad bright landscape; much I grieve
That, mingled with the toiling crowd, no more
I may return your varied views to mark,
Of rocks amid the sunshine towering dark,
Of rivers winding wild,[10] or mountains hoar,
Or castle gleaming on the distant steep!—
Yet many a look back on thy hills I cast,
And many a softened image of the past
Sadly combine, and bid remembrance keep,
To soothe me with fair scenes, and fancies rude,
When I pursue my path in solitude.

[10] There is a wildness almost fantastic in the view of the river from Stirling Castle, the course of which is seen for many miles, making a thousand turnings.

EVENING

Evening! as slow thy placid shades descend,
Veiling with gentlest hush the landscape still,
The lonely, battlement, the farthest hill
And wood, I think of those who have no friend;
Who now, perhaps, by melancholy led,
From the broad blaze of day, where pleasure flaunts,
Retiring, wander to the ring-dove's haunts
Unseen; and watch the tints that o'er thy bed
Hang lovely; oft to musing Fancy's eye
Presenting fairy vales, where the tired mind
Might rest beyond the murmurs of mankind,
Nor hear the hourly moans of misery!
Alas for man! that Hope's fair views the while
Should smile like you, and perish as they smile!

TO THE RIVER ITCHIN [11]

Itchin! when I behold thy banks again,
Thy crumbling margin, and thy silver breast,
On which the self-same tints still seem to rest,
Why feels my heart a shivering sense of pain!
Is it, that many a summer's day has past
Since, in life's morn, I carolled on thy side!
Is it, that oft since then my heart has sighed,
As Youth, and Hope's delusive gleams, flew fast!
Is it, that those who gathered on thy shore,
Companions of my youth, now meet no more!
Whate'er the cause, upon thy banks I bend,
Sorrowing; yet feel such solace at my heart,
As at the meeting of some long-lost friend,
From whom, in happier hours, we wept to part.

[11] The Itchin is a river running from Winchester to Southampton, the banks of which have been the scene of many a holiday sport. The lines were composed on an evening in a journey from Oxford to Southampton, the first time I had seen the Itchin since I left school.

ON RESIGNING A SCHOLARSHIP OF TRINITY COLLEGE, OXFORD, AND RETIRING TO A COUNTRY CURACY

Farewell! a long farewell! O Poverty,

Affection's fondest dream how hast thou reft!
But though, on thy stern brow no trace is left
Of youthful joys, that on the cold heart die,
With thee a sad companionship I seek,
Content, if poor;—for patient wretchedness,
Tearful, but uncomplaining of distress,
Who turns to the rude storm her faded cheek;
And Piety, who never told her wrong;
And calm Content, whose griefs no more rebel;
And Genius, warbling sweet, his saddest song,
When evening listens to some village knell,—
Long banished from the world's insulting throng;—
With thee, and thy unfriended children dwell.

DOVER CLIFFS

On these white cliffs, that calm above the flood
Uprear their shadowing heads, and at their feet
Hear not the surge that has for ages beat,
How many a lonely wanderer has stood!
And, whilst the lifted murmur met his ear,
And o'er the distant billows the still eve
Sailed slow, has thought of all his heart must leave
To-morrow; of the friends he loved most dear;
Of social scenes, from which he wept to part!
Oh! if, like me, he knew how fruitless all
The thoughts that would full fain the past recall,
Soon would he quell the risings of his heart,
And brave the wild winds and unhearing tide—
The World his country, and his GOD his guide.

ON LANDING AT OSTEND

The orient beam illumes the parting oar;—
From yonder azure track, emerging white,
The earliest sail slow gains upon the sight,
And the blue wave comes rippling to the shore.
Meantime far off the rear of darkness flies:
Yet 'mid the beauties of the morn, unmoved,
Like one for ever torn from all he loved,
Back o'er the deep I turn my longing eyes,
And chide the wayward passions that rebel:
Yet boots it not to think, or to complain,
Musing sad ditties to the reckless main.

To dreams like these, adieu! the pealing bell
Speaks of the hour that stays not—and the day
To life's sad turmoil calls my heart away.

1787.

THE BELLS, OSTEND [12]

How sweet the tuneful bells' responsive peal!
As when, at opening morn, the fragrant breeze
Breathes on the trembling sense of pale disease,
So piercing to my heart their force I feel!
And hark! with lessening cadence now they fall!
And now, along the white and level tide,
They fling their melancholy music wide;
Bidding me many a tender thought recall
Of summer-days, and those delightful years
When from an ancient tower, in life's fair prime,
The mournful magic of their mingling chime
First waked my wondering childhood into tears!
But seeming now, when all those days are o'er,
The sounds of joy once heard, and heard no more.

1787.

[12] Written on landing at Ostend, and hearing, very early in the morning, the carillons.

THE RHINE

'Twas morn, and beauteous on the mountain's brow
(Hung with the clusters of the bending vine)
Shone in the early light, when on the Rhine
We bounded, and the white waves round the prow
In murmurs parted:—varying as we go,
Lo! the woods open, and the rocks retire,
As some gray convent-wall or glistening spire
'Mid the bright landscape's track unfolding slow!
Here dark, with furrowed aspect, like Despair,
Frowns the bleak cliff! There on the woodland's side
The shadowy sunshine pours its streaming tide;
Whilst Hope, enchanted with the scene so fair,
Counts not the hours of a long summer's day,
Nor heeds how fast the prospect winds away.

INFLUENCE OF TIME ON GRIEF

O Time! who know'st a lenient hand to lay
Softest on Sorrow's wound, and slowly thence
(Lulling to sad repose the weary sense)
The faint pang stealest unperceived away;
On thee I rest my only hope at last,
And think, when thou hast dried the bitter tear
That flows in vain o'er all my soul held dear,
I may look back on every sorrow past,
And meet life's peaceful evening with a smile:—
As some lone bird, at day's departing hour,
Sings in the sunbeam, of the transient shower
Forgetful, though its wings are wet the while:—
Yet ah! how much must that poor heart endure,
Which hopes from thee, and thee alone, a cure!

THE CONVENT

If chance some pensive stranger, hither led,
His bosom glowing from majestic views,
Temple and tower 'mid the bright landscape's hues,
Should ask who sleeps beneath this lowly bed?
A maid of sorrow. To the cloistered scene,
Unknown and beautiful a mourner came,
Seeking with unseen tears to quench the flame
Of hapless love: yet was her look serene
As the pale moonlight in the midnight aisle;—
Her voice was gentle and a charm could lend,
Like that which spoke of a departed friend;
And a meek sadness sat upon her smile!—
Now, far removed from every earthly ill,
Her woes are buried, and her heart is still.

THE RIVER CHERWELL

Cherwell! how pleased along thy willowed edge
Erewhile I strayed, or when the morn began
To tinge the distant turret's golden fan,
Or evening glimmered o'er the sighing sedge!
And now reposing on thy banks once more,
I bid the lute farewell, and that sad lay

Whose music on my melancholy way
I wooed: beneath thy willows waving hoar,
Seeking a while to rest—till the bright sun
Of joy return; as when Heaven's radiant Bow
Beams on the night-storm's passing wings below:
Whate'er betide, yet something have I won
Of solace, that may bear me on serene,
Till eve's last hush shall close the silent scene.

ON ENTERING SWITZERLAND

Languid, and sad, and slow, from day to day
I journey on, yet pensive turn to view,
Where the rich landscape gleams with softer hue,
The streams, and vales, and hills, that steal away.
So fares it with the children of the earth:
For when life's goodly prospect opens round,
Their spirits burn to tread that fairy ground,
Where every vale sounds to the pipe of mirth.
But them, alas! the dream of youth beguiles,
And soon a longing look, like me, they cast
Back on the mountains of the morning past:
Yet Hope still beckons us, and beckoning smiles,
And to a brighter world her view extends,
When earth's long darkness on her path descends.

DISTANT VIEW OF ENGLAND FROM THE SEA

Yes! from mine eyes the tears unbidden start,
As thee, my country, and the long-lost sight
Of thy own cliffs, that lift their summits white
Above the wave, once more my beating heart
With eager hope and filial transport hails!
Scenes of my youth, reviving gales ye bring,
As when erewhile the tuneful morn of spring
Joyous awoke amidst your hawthorn vales,
And filled with fragrance every village lane:
Fled are those hours, and all the joys they gave!
Yet still I gaze, and count each rising wave
That bears me nearer to my home again;
If haply, 'mid those woods and vales so fair,
Stranger to Peace, I yet may meet her there.

HOPE

As one who, long by wasting sickness worn,
Weary has watched the lingering night, and heard
Unmoved the carol of the matin bird
Salute his lonely porch; now first at morn
Goes forth, leaving his melancholy bed;
He the green slope and level meadow views,
Delightful bathed with slow-ascending dews;
Or marks the clouds, that o'er the mountain's head
In varying forms fantastic wander white;
Or turns his ear to every random song,
Heard the green river's winding marge along,
The whilst each sense is steeped in still delight.
So o'er my breast young Summer's breath I feel,
Sweet Hope! thy fragrance pure and healing incense steal!

TO A FRIEND

Go, then, and join the murmuring city's throng!
Me thou dost leave to solitude and tears;
To busy phantasies, and boding fears,
Lest ill betide thee; but 'twill not be long
Ere the hard season shall be past; till then
Live happy; sometimes the forsaken shade
Remembering, and these trees now left to fade;
Nor, 'mid the busy scenes and hum of men,
Wilt thou my cares forget: in heaviness
To me the hours shall roll, weary and slow,
Till mournful autumn past, and all the snow
Of winter pale, the glad hour I shall bless
That shall restore thee from the crowd again,
To the green hamlet on the peaceful plain.

1792.

ABSENCE

There is strange music in the stirring wind,
When lowers the autumnal eve, and all alone
To the dark wood's cold covert thou art gone,
Whose ancient trees on the rough slope reclined
Rock, and at times scatter their tresses sere.

If in such shades, beneath their murmuring,
Thou late hast passed the happier hours of spring,
With sadness thou wilt mark the fading year;
Chiefly if one, with whom such sweets at morn
Or evening thou hast shared, afar shall stray.
O Spring, return! return, auspicious May!
But sad will be thy coming, and forlorn,
If she return not with thy cheering ray,
Who from these shades is gone, far, far away.

BEREAVEMENT

Whose was that gentle voice, that, whispering sweet,
Promised methought long days of bliss sincere!
Soothing it stole on my deluded ear,
Most like soft music, that might sometimes cheat
Thoughts dark and drooping! 'Twas the voice of Hope.
Of love, and social scenes, it seemed to speak,
Of truth, of friendship, of affection meek;
That, oh! poor friend, might to life's downward slope
Lead us in peace, and bless our latest hours.
Ah me! the prospect saddened as she sung;
Loud on my startled ear the death-bell rung;
Chill darkness wrapt the pleasurable bowers,
Whilst Horror, pointing to yon breathless clay,
"No peace be thine," exclaimed, "away, away!"

1793.

OXFORD REVISITED

I never hear the sound of thy glad bells,
Oxford, and chime harmonious, but I say,
Sighing to think how time has worn away,
Some spirit speaks in the sweet tone that swells,
Heard after years of absence, from the vale
Where Cherwell winds. Most true it speaks the tale
Of days departed, and its voice recalls
Hours of delight and hope in the gay tide
Of life, and many friends now scattered wide
By many fates. Peace be within thy walls!
I have scarce heart to visit thee; but yet,
Denied the joys sought in thy shades,—denied
Each better hope, since my poor Harriet died,

What I have owed to thee, my heart can ne'er forget!

IN MEMORIAM

How blessed with thee the path could I have trod
Of quiet life, above cold want's hard fate,
(And little wishing more) nor of the great
Envious, or their proud name; but it pleased GOD
To take thee to his mercy: thou didst go
In youth and beauty to thy cold death-bed;
Even whilst on dreams of bliss we fondly fed,
Of years to come of comfort! Be it so.
Ere this I have felt sorrow; and even now,
Though sometimes the unbidden tear will start,
And half unman the miserable heart,
The cold dew I shall wipe from my sad brow,
And say, since hopes of bliss on earth are vain,
Best friend, farewell, till we do meet again!

ON THE DEATH OF THE REV. WILLIAM BENWELL, M.A. [13]

Thou camest with kind looks, when on the brink
Almost of death I strove, and with mild voice
Didst soothe me, bidding my poor heart rejoice,
Though smitten sore: Oh, I did little think
That thou, my friend, wouldst the first victim fall
To the stern King of Terrors! Thou didst fly,
By pity prompted, at the poor man's cry;
And soon thyself were stretched beneath the pall,
Livid infection's prey. The deep distress
Of her, who best thy inmost bosom knew,
To whom thy faith was vowed; thy soul was true,
What powers of faltering language shall express?
As friendship bids, I feebly breathe my own,
And sorrowing say, Pure spirit, thou art gone!

[13] An accomplished young friend of the author—a poet and a scholar, formerly fellow of Trinity College, Oxford—who died of a typhus fever, caught in administering the sacrament to one of his parishioners. Mr Benwell had only been married eleven weeks when he died.

AT MALVERN

I shall behold far off thy towering crest,
Proud mountain! from thy heights as slow I stray
Down through the distant vale my homeward way,
I shall behold upon thy rugged breast,
The parting sun sit smiling: me the while
Escaped the crowd, thoughts full of heaviness
May visit, as life's bitter losses press
Hard on my bosom; but I shall beguile
The thing I am, and think, that ev'n as thou
Dost lift in the pale beam thy forehead high,
Proud mountain! whilst the scattered vapours fly
Unheeded round thy breast,—so, with calm brow,
The shades of sorrow I may meet, and wear
The smile unchanged of peace, though pressed by care!

NETLEY ABBEY

Fall'n pile! I ask not what has been thy fate;
But when the winds, slow wafted from the main,
Through each rent arch, like spirits that complain,
Come hollow to my ear, I meditate
On this world's passing pageant, and the lot
Of those who once majestic in their prime
Stood smiling at decay, till bowed by time
Or injury, their early boast forgot,
They may have fall'n like thee! Pale and forlorn,
Their brow, besprent with thin hairs, white as snow,
They lift, still unsubdued, as they would scorn
This short-lived scene of vanity and woe;
Whilst on their sad looks smilingly they bear
The trace of creeping age, and the pale hue of care!

ASSOCIATIONS

As o'er these hills I take my silent rounds,
Still on that vision which is flown I dwell,
On images I loved, alas, too well!
Now past, and but remembered like sweet sounds
Of yesterday! Yet in my breast I keep
Such recollections, painful though they seem,
And hours of joy retrace, till from my dream
I start, and find them not; then I could weep
To think how Fortune blights the fairest flowers;
To think how soon life's first endearments fail,

And we are still misled by Hope's smooth tale,
Who, like a flatterer, when the happiest hours
Pass, and when most we call on her to stay,
Will fly, as faithless and as fleet as they!

MUSIC

O harmony! thou tenderest nurse of pain,
If that thy note's sweet magic e'er can heal
Griefs which the patient spirit oft may feel,
Oh! let me listen to thy songs again;
Till memory her fairest tints shall bring;
Hope wake with brighter eye, and listening seem
With smiles to think on some delightful dream,
That waved o'er the charmed sense its gladsome wing!
For when thou leadest all thy soothing strains
More smooth along, the silent passions meet
In one suspended transport, sad and sweet;
And nought but sorrow's softest touch remains;
That, when the transitory charm is o'er,
Just wakes a tear, and then is felt no more.

APPROACH OF SUMMER

How shall I meet thee, Summer, wont to fill
My heart with gladness, when thy pleasant tide
First came, and on the Coomb's romantic side
Was heard the distant cuckoo's hollow bill!
Fresh flowers shall fringe the margin of the stream,
As with the songs of joyance and of hope
The hedge-rows shall ring loud, and on the slope
The poplars sparkle in the passing beam;
The shrubs and laurels that I loved to tend,
Thinking their May-tide fragrance would delight,
With many a peaceful charm, thee, my poor friend,
Shall put forth their green shoots, and cheer the sight!
But I shall mark their hues with sadder eyes,
And weep the more for one who in the cold earth lies!

AT OXFORD, 1786

Bereave me not of Fancy's shadowy dreams,

Which won my heart, or when the gay career
Of life begun, or when at times a tear
Sat sad on memory's cheek—though loftier themes
Await the awakened mind to the high prize
Of wisdom, hardly earned with toil and pain,
Aspiring patient; yet on life's wide plain
Left fatherless, where many a wanderer sighs
Hourly, and oft our road is lone and long,
'Twere not a crime should we a while delay
Amid the sunny field; and happier they
Who, as they journey, woo the charm of song,
To cheer their way;—till they forget to weep,
And the tired sense is hushed, and sinks to sleep.

AT DOVER, 1786

Thou, whose stern spirit loves the storm,
That, borne on Terror's desolating wings,
Shakes the high forest, or remorseless flings
The shivered surge; when rising griefs deform
Thy peaceful breast, hie to yon steep, and think,—
When thou dost mark the melancholy tide
Beneath thee, and the storm careering wide,—
Tossed on the surge of life how many sink!
And if thy cheek with one kind tear be wet,
And if thy heart be smitten, when the cry
Of danger and of death is heard more nigh,
Oh, learn thy private sorrows to forget;
Intent, when hardest beats the storm, to save
One who, like thee, has suffered from the wave.

RETROSPECTION

I turn these leaves with thronging thoughts, and say,
Alas! how many friends of youth are dead;
How many visions of fair hope have fled,
Since first, my Muse, we met.—So speeds away
Life, and its shadows; yet we sit and sing,
Stretched in the noontide bower, as if the day
Declined not, and we yet might trill our lay
Beneath the pleasant morning's purple wing
That fans us; while aloft the gay clouds shine!
Oh, ere the coming of the long cold night,
Religion, may we bless thy purer light,

That still shall warm us, when the tints decline
O'er earth's dim hemisphere; and sad we gaze
On the vain visions of our passing days!

ON ACCIDENTALLY MEETING A LADY NOW NO MORE

WRITTEN MANY YEARS AFTER THE FOREGOING SONNETS

When last we parted, thou wert young and fair—
How beautiful let fond remembrance say!
Alas! since then old Time has stol'n away
Nigh forty years, leaving my temples bare:—
So hath it perished, like a thing of air,
That dream of love and youth:—we now are gray;
Yet still remembering youth's enchanted way,
Though time has changed my look, and blanched my hair,
Though I remember one sad hour with pain,
And never thought, long as I yet might live,
And parted long, to hear that voice again;—
I can a sad, but cordial greeting, give,
And for thy welfare breathe as warm a prayer,
Lady, as when I loved thee young and fair!

ON HEARING "THE MESSIAH" PERFORMED IN GLOUCESTER CATHEDRAL, SEPT. 18, 1835

Oh, stay, harmonious and sweet sounds, that die
In the long vaultings of this ancient fane!
Stay, for I may not hear on earth again
Those pious airs—that glorious harmony;
Lifting the soul to brighter orbs on high,
Worlds without sin or sorrow!
Ah, the strain
Has died—ev'n the last sounds that lingeringly
Hung on the roof ere they expired!
And I,
Stand in the world of strife, amidst a throng,
A throng that recks not or of death, or sin!
Oh, jarring scenes! to cease, indeed, ere long;
The worm hears not the discord and the din;
But he whose heart thrills to this angel song,
Feels the pure joy of heaven on earth begin!

WOODSPRING ABBEY, 1836.[14]

These walls were built by men who did a deed
Of blood:—terrific conscience, day by day,
Followed, where'er their shadow seemed to stay,
And still in thought they saw their victim bleed,
Before God's altar shrieking: pangs succeed,
As dire upon their heart the deep sin lay,
No tears of agony could wash away:
Hence! to the land's remotest limit, speed!
These walls are raised in vain, as vainly flows
Contrition's tear: Earth, hide them, and thou, Sea,
Which round the lone isle, where their bones repose,
Dost sound for ever, their sad requiem be,
In fancy's ear, at pensive evening's close,
Still murmuring MISERERE, DOMINE.

[14] *Three mailed men, in Canterbury Cathedral, rushed on the Archbishop of Canterbury, and murdered him before the altar. Conscience-stricken, they fled and built Woodspring Abbey, in the remote corner of Somersetshire, near Western Super Mare, where the land looks on the Atlantic sea. There are three unknown graves on the Flat Holms.*

LACOCK NUNNERY. JUNE 24, 1837

I stood upon the stone where ELA lay,
The widowed founder of these ancient walls,
Where fancy still on meek devotion calls,
Marking the ivied arch, and turret gray—
For her soul's rest—eternal rest—to pray;[15]
Where visionary nuns yet seem to tread,
A pale dim troop, the cloisters of the dead,
Though twice three hundred years have flown away!
But when, with silent step and pensive mien,
In weeds, as mourning for her sisters gone,
The mistress of this lone monastic scene
Came; and I heard her voice's tender tone,
I said, Though centuries have rolled between,
One gentle, beauteous nun is left, on earth, alone.

[15] *"Eternam Requiem dona."*

ON A BEAUTIFUL LANDSCAPE

Beautiful landscape! I could look on thee

For hours, unmindful of the storm and strife,
And mingled murmurs of tumultuous life.
Here, all is still as fair; the stream, the tree,
The wood, the sunshine on the bank: no tear,
No thought of Time's swift wing, or closing night,
That comes to steal away the long sweet light—
No sighs of sad humanity are here.
Here is no tint of mortal change; the day,—
Beneath whose light the dog and peasant-boy
Gambol, with look, and almost bark, of joy,—
Still seems, though centuries have passed, to stay.
Then gaze again, that shadowed scenes may teach
Lessons of peace and love, beyond all speech.

ART AND NATURE. THE BRIDGE BETWEEN CLIFTON AND LEIGH WOODS

Frown ever opposite, the angel cried,
Who, with an earthquake's might and giant hand,
Severed these riven rocks, and bade them stand
Severed for ever! The vast ocean-tide,
Leaving its roar without at his command,
Shrank, and beneath the woods through the green land
Went gently murmuring on, so to deride
The frowning barriers that its force defied!
But Art, high o'er the trailing smoke below
Of sea-bound steamer, on yon summit's head
Sat musing; and where scarce a wandering crow
Sailed o'er the chasm, in thought a highway led;
Conquering, as by an arrow from a bow,
The scene's lone Genius by her elfin-thread.

CLIFTON, 27th August 1836.

PICTURE OF AN OLD MAN

Old man, I saw thee in thy garden chair
Sitting in silence 'mid the shrubs and trees
Of thy small cottage-croft, whilst murmuring bees
Went by, and almost touched thy temples bare,
Edged with a few flakes of the whitest hair.
And, soothed by the faint hum of ebbing seas,
And song of birds, and breath of the young breeze,
Thus didst thou sit, feeling the summer air
Blow gently;—with a sad still decadence,

Sinking to earth in hope, but all alone.
Oh! hast thou wept to feel the lonely sense
Of earthly loss, musing on voices gone!
Hush the vain murmur, that, without offence,
Thy head may rest in peace beneath the churchyard stone.

PICTURE OF A YOUNG LADY

When I was sitting, sad, and all alone,
Remembering youth and love for ever fled,
And many friends now resting with the dead,
While the still summer's light departing shone,
Like many sweet and silent summers gone;
Thou camest, as a vision, with a mien
And smile like those I once on earth had seen,
And with a voice of that remembered tone
Which I in other days, long since, had heard:
Like Peace approaching, when distempers fret
Most the tired spirit, thy fair form appeared;
And till I die, I never shall forget,—
For at thy footstep light, the gloom was cheered,—
Thy look and voice, oh! gentle Margaret.

HOUR-GLASS AND BIBLE

Look, Christian, on thy Bible, and that glass
That sheds its sand through minutes, hours, and days,
And years; it speaks not, yet, methinks, it says,
To every human heart: so mortals pass
On to their dark and silent grave! Alas
For man! an exile upon earth he strays,
Weary, and wandering through benighted ways;
To-day in strength, to-morrow like the grass
That withers at his feet!—Lift up thy head,
Poor pilgrim, toiling in this vale of tears;
That book declares whose blood for thee was shed,
Who died to give thee life; and though thy years
Pass like a shade, pointing to thy death-bed,
Out of the deep thy cry an angel hears,
And by his guiding hand thy steps to heaven are led!

MILTON. ON THE BUSTS OF MILTON, IN YOUTH AND AGE, AT STOURHEAD

IN YOUTH

Milton, our noblest poet, in the grace
Of youth, in those fair eyes and clustering hair,
That brow untouched by one faint line of care,
To mar its openness, we seem to trace
The front of the first lord of human race,
'Mid thine own Paradise portrayed so fair,
Ere Sin or Sorrow scathed it: such the air
That characters thy youth. Shall time efface
These lineaments as crowding cares assail!
It is the lot of fall'n humanity.
What boots it! armed in adamantine mail,
The unconquerable mind, and genius high,
Right onward hold their way through weal and woe,
Or whether life's brief lot be high or low!

IN AGE

And art thou he, now "fall'n on evil days,"
And changed indeed! Yet what do this sunk cheek,
These thinner locks, and that calm forehead speak!
A spirit reckless of man's blame or praise,—
A spirit, when thine eyes to the noon's blaze
Their dark orbs roll in vain, in suffering meek,
As in the sight of God intent to seek,
'Mid solitude or age, or through the ways
Of hard adversity, the approving look
Of its great Master; whilst the conscious pride
Of wisdom, patient and content to brook
All ills to that sole Master's task applied,
Shall show before high heaven the unaltered mind,
Milton, though thou art poor, and old, and blind!

TO SIR WALTER SCOTT

ON ACCIDENTLY MEETING AND PARTING WITH SIR WALTER SCOTT, WHOM I HAD NOT SEEN FOR
MANY YEARS, IN THE STREETS OF LONDON, MAY 1828

Since last I saw that countenance so mild,
Slow-stealing age, and a faint line of care,
Had gently touched, methought, some features there;
Yet looked the man as placid as a child,
And the same voice,—whilst mingled with the throng,

Unknowing, and unknown, we passed along,—
That voice, a share of the brief time beguiled!
That voice I ne'er may hear again, I sighed
At parting,—wheresoe'er our various way,
In this great world,—but from the banks of Tweed,
As slowly sink the shades of eventide,
Oh! I shall hear the music of his reed,
Far off, and thinking of that voice, shall say,
A blessing rest upon thy locks of gray!

William Lisle Bowles – A Short Biography

William Lisle Bowles was born on 24th September 1762 at King's Sutton in Northamptonshire.

His great-grandfather, grandfather and his father, William Thomas Bowles, had all been parish priests and inevitably Bowles would join their line.

At the age of 14 he entered Winchester College, where the headmaster was Dr Joseph Warton (a minor poet, his most notable piece is The Enthusiast, 1744. In 1755, he taught at Winchester and from 1766 to 1793 was headmaster. His career as a critic was illustrious. He produced editions of poets such as Virgil as well as several English poets).

In 1789 Bowles published, a small quarto volume, Fourteen Sonnets, which was received with extraordinary praise, not only by the general public, but by such revered poets as Samuel Taylor Coleridge and Wordsworth.

The Sonnets were a return to an older and purer poetic style, and by their grace of expression, lyrical versification, tender tone of feeling and vivid appreciation of the wonder and beauty of nature, stood out in marked contrast to the elaborate works which then formed the bulk of English poetry.

Bowles said "Poetic trifles from solitary rambles whilst chewing the cud of sweet and bitter fancy, written from memory, confined to fourteen lines, this seemed best adapted to the unity of sentiment, the verse flowed in unpremeditated harmony as my ear directed but are far from being mere elegiac couplets".

The young Samuel Taylor Coleridge felt obliged to record his debt of gratitude to Bowles: "My obligations to Mr. Bowles were indeed important, and for radical good. At a very premature age, ... I had bewildered myself in metaphysicks, and in theological controversy. Nothing else pleased me. Poetry ... became insipid to me.... This preposterous pursuit was, beyond doubt, injurious both to my natural powers, and to the progress of my education.... But from this I was auspiciously withdrawn, chiefly by the genial influence of a style of poetry, so tender and yet so manly, so natural and real, and yet so dignified and harmonious, as the sonnets &c. of Mr. Bowles!"

In 1781 Bowles left as captain of Winchester school, and proceeded to Trinity College, Oxford, after winning a scholarship. Two years later he won the Chancellor's prize for Latin verse. It was now evident that the Church and poetry were to be his two callings.

After receiving his degree at Oxford, Bowles now began his career in service to the Church of England. In 1792, after serving as curate in Donhead St Andrew, Bowles was appointed vicar of Chicklade in Wiltshire.

Five years later, in 1797, he received the vicarage of Dumbleton in Gloucestershire, and in 1804 became vicar of Bremhill in Wiltshire, where he wrote the poem seen on Maud Heath's statue. In the same year his bishop, John Douglas, collated him to a prebendal stall in Salisbury Cathedral.

In 1818 Bowles was made chaplain to the Prince Regent, and in 1828 he was elected residentiary canon of Salisbury.

His years of service perhaps diminished both his stature as a poet and certainly the way he was viewed. For much of his career Bowles was seen as rather soft when set against his contemporaries but in the end his ability as a poet was enshrined, after a long and ferocious attack against him, by the principles he so eloquently wrote about and adhered too.

It is as well to remember that when critics suggest that compared to other poets his longer works were not to the standard that the competition achieved, that this era is perhaps without poetic equal. Set against Byron, Shelley, Keats, Wordsworth and other great luminaries of the era it is perhaps difficult to see his works in isolation for their own value.

The longer poems published by Bowles are distinguished by purity of imagination, cultured and graceful diction, and a great thoughtfulness of feeling. Among them were The Spirit of Discovery (1804), which alas was so mercilessly ridiculed by Byron; The Missionary (1813); The Grave of the Last Saxon (1822); and St John in Patmos (1833).

In 1806 he published an edition of Alexander Pope's works with notes and an essay, in which he laid down certain canons as to poetic imagery which, subject to some modification, were later accepted, but received at the time with strong opposition by admirers of Pope.

Bowles restated his views in 1819, in The Invariable Principles of Poetry. The controversy brought into sharp contrast the opposing views of poetry, which may be thought of as being either the natural or the artificial.

In personality and nature Bowles was said to be an amiable, absent-minded, but rather eccentric man. His poems speak warmly of a refinement of feeling, tenderness, and pensive thought, but are lacking in power and passion. But that should not diminish their value or appreciation to us.

Bowles maintained that images drawn from nature are poetically finer than those drawn from art; and that in the highest kinds of poetry the themes or passions handled should be of the general or elemental kind, and not the transient manners of any society. These positions were attacked by Byron, Thomas Campbell, William Roscoe and others, and for a time Bowles had to fight his corner on his own. Soon however, William Hazlitt and the Blackwood critics came to his assistance, and on the whole Bowles had reason to congratulate himself on having established certain principles which might serve as the basis of a true method of poetical criticism, and of having inaugurated, both by precept and by example, a new era in English poetry.

As well as his poetry Bowles was also responsible for writing a Life of Bishop Ken (in two volumes, 1830–1831), Coombe Ellen and St. Michael's Mount (1798), The Battle of the Nile (1799), and The Sorrows of Switzerland (1801).

Bowles also enjoyed considerable reputation as an antiquary and his principal work in that field was Hermes Britannicus (1828).

William Lisle Bowles died on April 7th, 1850 at the age of 87.

www.ingramcontent.com/pod-product-compliance
Lightning Source LLC
Chambersburg PA
CBHW070113070426
42448CB00038B/2660